P9-CDC-467

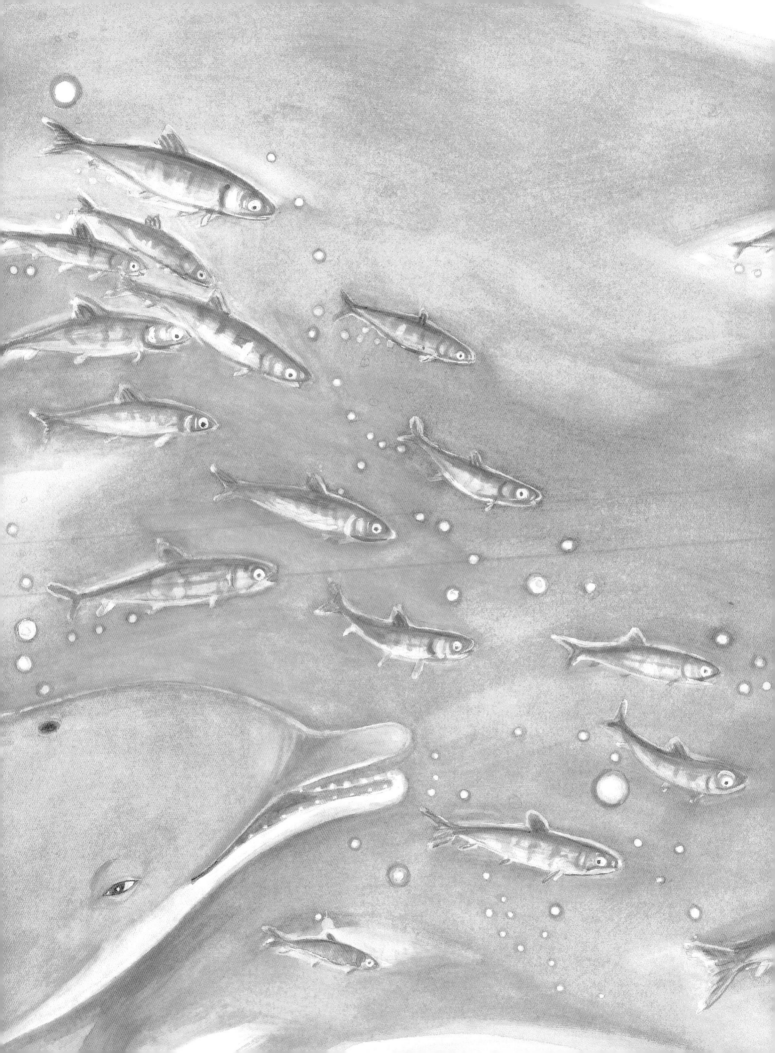

BUBBLE HOMES
and FISH FARTS

Fiona Bayrock

Illustrated by
Carolyn Conahan

Charlesbridge

For my mom, to whom I owe countless bottles of dish soap
and many summer days filled with bubble-chasing laughter.
With love—F. B.

To my mom, Katharine R. Digby, and Pat Robertson, and
great science teachers everywhere, for passing along their
interest in all things interesting, which is everything,
more or less—C. C.

Text copyright © 2009 by Fiona Bayrock
Illustrations copyright © 2009 by Carolyn Conahan
All rights reserved, including the right of reproduction in whole or in part in any form.
Charlesbridge and colophon are registered trademarks of Charlesbridge Publishing, Inc.

Published by Charlesbridge
85 Main Street
Watertown, MA 02472
(617) 926-0329
www.charlesbridge.com

Library of Congress Cataloging-in-Publication Data
Bayrock, Fiona.
   Bubble homes and fish farts / Fiona Bayrock; illustrated by
Carolyn Conahan.
      p. cm.
   ISBN 978-1-57091-669-4 (reinforced for library use)
   ISBN 978-1-57091-670-0 (softcover)
1. Animals—Juvenile literature. 2. Bubbles—Juvenile literature.
I. Conahan, Carolyn, ill. II. Title.
QL49.B39 2009
590—dc22

Printed in China
(hc) 10 9 8 7 6 5 4 3 2 1
(sc) 10 9 8 7 6 5 4 3 2 1

Illustrations done in watercolor on 140-lb. extra-white hot-press Fabriano Artistico paper
Display type set in Flora Dora, designed by Nick Curtis
Text type set in Goudy, designed by Frederic W. Goudy
Color separations by Chroma Graphics, Singapore
Printed and bound by Regent Publishing Services
Production supervision by Brian G. Walker
Designed by Susan Mallory Sherman

Bubbles are soft and squishy and full of air. They shimmer. They float. And they are very handy. Animals make bubbles, ride bubbles, breathe bubbles, and even live in bubbles. Animals use bubbles in amazing ways.

BUBBLES ARE FOR SAILING.

Violet Sea Snail • *Janthina janthina*

Violet sea snails can't swim. Instead, they sail along the ocean surface on rafts made of bubbles. First, a snail oozes a blob of bubbles that hardens. Then the snail hangs upside down from its floating bubble raft. It drifts with the wind and the currents, feeding on small surface animals it happens to find. The bubble raft doesn't break, because the snails are lightweight, thanks to their paper-thin shells and small size—about the size of a large grape. Very few shelled animals live at the surface. This means violet sea snails can feast on food that most shelled ocean animals can't reach.

9

BUBBLES ARE FOR RUNNING.

Water Shrew • *Sorex palustris*

With a name like "water shrew," it's no surprise that this tiny mammal is an expert swimmer. Over and over, it dives to the bottoms of mountain lakes and streams, searching for insect nymphs and small fish to eat. Many water-loving animals have webbed feet to help them swim. The water shrew has hind feet that work like swim fins, but they aren't webbed. Instead, they have a fringe of rigid hairs around each toe that does the job. The hairs also trap air bubbles under the feet—enough that the shrew can actually run on top of the water for several seconds at a time.

No, it's not
a miracle.
But it is a very
good trick!

Upside-down is right-side-up for me!

BUBBLES ARE FOR BREATHING.

Backswimmer • *Notonecta glauca*

Like scuba divers, backswimmer bugs take two containers of air underwater with them so they can breathe. The backswimmer's air containers are pockets on its body. Clinging upside down to an underwater plant, the backswimmer looks up for mosquito larvae, small tadpoles, and other unsuspecting prey. When something tasty comes along, the backswimmer's bubbles carry it up for the attack. It can also chase prey by paddling long, powerful hind legs like boat oars. Backswimmers can stay underwater for hours before riding their bubbles to the surface for fresh air.

BUBBLES ARE FOR KEEPING WARM.

Sea Otter • *Enhydra lutris*

Sea otters spend their lives in cold ocean water—swimming, floating, diving for food, eating, having babies, and even sleeping. Most sea mammals have a thick layer of fat under the skin to protect them from the cold. Otters don't. So how do they stay warm? Bubbles to the rescue! Sea otters blow bubbles and whisk the water to make even more bubbles. Then they rub the bubbles into their fur. Sea otter hairs are shaped to "zip lock" together to keep air bubbles in and cold water out. The layer of air trapped in the dense underhair works like a down comforter to help sea otters stay warm.

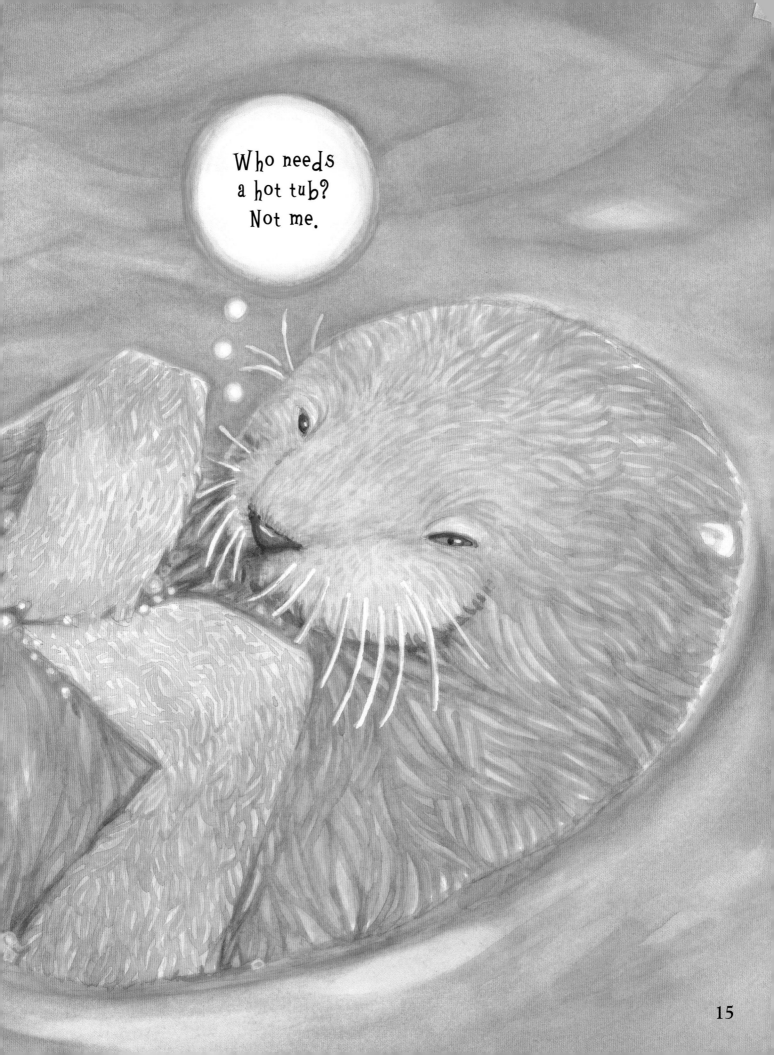

15

BUBBLES ARE FOR LIVING IN.

Water Spider • *Argyroneta aquatica*

Water spiders weave their webs underwater. New webs look like little trampolines attached to underwater plants. Once a web is complete, the spider dives from the surface with tiny air bubbles clinging to its hairy body. It shakes and scrapes them loose under the web. The bubbles float upward and get caught in the web. The spider keeps diving with more bubbles until a big bubble forms from the smaller ones. The bubble pushes the web upward so it looks like a bell. The spider then lives inside the bubble. It breathes the bubble air as it looks for prey, eats, mates, lays eggs, and hibernates.

I smell
something
yummy.

18

BUBBLES ARE FOR FINDING FOOD.

Star-nosed Mole • *Condylura cristata*

The star-nosed mole feels and smells its way underground and underwater. The fleshy star nose works like a bunch of super fingers, touching, touching, here, there, and everywhere, searching for something good to eat. Star-nosed moles also have a good sense of smell, even when underwater. As it swims, a mole blows bubbles from its nose and breathes them back in. A quick sniff of the bubble air tells the mole if lunch is nearby and which way to go to find it. Fish and worms—yummy meals for a star-nosed mole— leave underwater scent trails. These scents in the water mix with the bubble air. Swimming moles sniff to follow scent trails underwater just as dogs do on land.

Not me!

Not me!

19

BUBBLES ARE FOR SAVING ANIMALS.

Human • *Homo sapiens*

Clang! A huge hammer pounds a long steel tube into the bottom of San Francisco Bay. Each tube, called a pile, measures eight feet across and is longer than a football field (330 feet, or 100 meters). The new Bay Bridge will be built on more than one hundred of these piles. Clang! Above the water, it sounds like a giant church bell, but under the water, the sound waves are powerful enough to kill nearby fish. Each pile is pounded thousands of times. That's a lot of dead fish. Construction crews use bubbles to save the fish. They pump air into plastic piping placed around the pile. The air flows through holes in the piping and streams in bubbles to the surface. The curtain of bubbles stops dangerous sound waves from reaching the fish.

More amazing facts about
BUBBLE MAKERS

Snail? What snail?

Violet Sea Snail • *Janthina janthina*
Habitat: Warm ocean surfaces
Where: Worldwide • Size across: 1 inch (3 cm)
Amazing Fact: When sailing on their bubble rafts, violet sea snails are purple on top and almost white on the bottom. This difference in top and bottom color is called countershading. Thanks to countershading, the snails are able to hide out in the open. The darker side blends into the color of the water as seen by birds from the air, while the white side blends into the sunlight as seen by predators from underneath.

So ... these pictures aren't to scale?

Water Shrew • *Sorex palustris*
Habitat: Edges of streams and lakes in forested mountain areas
Where: Southern Alaska, west and northeast U.S.,
most of southern Canada • Length: 6 inches (15 cm)
Amazing Facts: As the water shrew dives, a silvery layer of bubbles covers its body, so it must swim hard to reach the bottom. Shrews that stop paddling pop up to the surface like a cork. An adult water shrew weighs about as much as three U.S. nickels, which makes this shrew the smallest of all diving mammals.

Backswimmer • *Notonecta glauca*
Habitat: Ponds, lake edges, small pools, and other still freshwater
Where: Europe • Length: 0.5 inches (1.3 cm)
Amazing Facts: Hairs on the backswimmer's feet, joints, and lower body sense when prey is moving nearby. Backswimmers know which movements are made by something good to eat and which aren't. Backswimmers also have wings, so if a pool or pond dries up, they simply fly to a new one, grab more bubbles from the surface, and dive in.

Maybe they are. Maybe we grew!

Dream on.

Sea Otter • *Enhydra lutris*
Habitat: Ocean
Where: North Pacific • Body length: 40 inches (1 m)

Amazing Facts: Until sea otter pups learn to groom bubbles into their own fur, the mother keeps her pups dry by carrying them on her belly as she floats on her back. Sea otters drift when they're asleep, so sometimes a sea otter will use strands of kelp to anchor itself like a boat. Sea otters have the densest fur of any animal—up to one million hairs per square inch (6.45 square cm).

Water Spider • *Argyroneta aquatica*
Habitat: Still or slow-moving freshwater
Where: Northern and central Europe, Siberia, northern Asia
Length: 0.5 inches (1.3 cm)

Amazing Facts: This is the only spider that spends its whole life underwater. Sitting in its bubble home, it pokes its legs into the water below. When its legs detect prey moving nearby or struggling on the surface, the spider leaves the bubble and pounces. It then brings the prey back to the bubble to eat.

Star-nosed Mole • *Condylura cristata*
Habitat: Wetlands
Where: Eastern Canada, northeastern United States
Body length: 4.5 inches (11 cm)

I smell something BIG.

Amazing Fact: Star-nosed moles breathe bubbles in and out very fast—between five and ten times per second. That's about the same sniffing rate as similar land animals, such as rats and mice.

Humpback Whale • *Megaptera novaeangliae*
Habitat: Ocean
Where: Worldwide, except Arabian Gulf; Mediterranean, Baltic, and Red Seas; and extreme polar regions • Length: 45 feet (14 m)

Amazing Facts: For humpbacks, fishing with bubble nets is almost like a dance. Each whale performs the same moves with each net. One calls, others make the bubble net, and all of the whales leap out of the water in exactly the same order and location, lunge after lunge. You can tell humpback whales apart by looking at their tail markings. No two are the same.

Weddell Seal • *Leptonychotes weddellii*
Habitat: Cold ocean, sea ice
Where: Antarctic • Length: 10 feet (3 m)

Amazing Facts: A Weddell seal can stay underwater for more than an hour at a time, dive ten times deeper than scuba divers can go, and eat hundreds of fish per day. Watching the first seal-cam videos, scientists were surprised to learn that Weddell seals use bubbles to chase fish. These seals also blow bubbles to keep other seals from stealing their breathing holes.

Herring
***Clupea pallasii* (Pacific); *Clupea harengus* (Atlantic)**
Habitat: Ocean, near the coast
Where: (Atlantic herring) North Atlantic, North Sea, Baltic Sea; (Pacific herring) North Pacific • Length: up to 16 inches (40 cm)

Amazing Fact: Herring FaRTs were discovered by accident. When researchers heard the noise coming from a lab down the hall, they thought the fish scientists were being rude. The fish scientists thought the researchers were playing a joke on them—until they realized the sounds were coming from a herring tank in which someone had left the microphone turned on.

Snapping Shrimp • *Alpheus heterochaelis*
Habitat: Shallow tropical and subtropical ocean waters, coral reefs
Where: Worldwide • Length: 2 inches (5 cm)

Amazing Facts: These pinkie-sized shrimp have one claw that is much larger than the other. This claw makes bubbles. Each collapsing bubble makes a short, bright flash of light and bit of extreme heat—up to 36,000° F (20,000° C). That's hotter than the surface of the sun! Next time you're snorkeling and you hear the sound of popcorn popping, look for a colony of snapping shrimp.

Bottlenose Dolphin • *Tursiops truncatus*
Habitat: Ocean • Where: Worldwide, except in polar regions
Length: 6 to 13 feet (2 to 4 m)

Amazing Facts: Dolphins learn from other dolphins how to make bubble rings. It takes practice to get it right. Some dolphins can send bubble rings traveling in different directions, make one bubble ring by joining two rings together, or make a ring larger by adding more air. Scientists haven't found a practical reason for the bubble rings. Dolphins appear to make them just for fun.

Rattlebox Moth • *Utetheisa ornatrix*
Habitat: Forest edges, fields
Where: North America (east of Arizona, south of Ontario) to
northern South America, Bermuda, Bahamas, Greater Antilles
Wingspan: 1.5 inches (4 cm)

Amazing Facts: The yucky-tasting chemical made by the rattlebox moth is
called pyrrolizidine alkaloid, or PA, for short. It protects the eggs from ants and
ladybugs, as well as protecting the larvae and adult moths from spiders. Female
rattlebox moths prefer mates that have a large amount of PA.

Western Spittlebug • *Clastoptera juniperina*
Habitat: Juniper trees and shrubs
Where: North America (Rocky Mountains and west)
Length: 0.34 inches (1 cm)

Amazing Facts: It takes 15 to 30 minutes for a spittlebug to make enough
bubbles to completely cover its body. Spittlebugs don't usually cause serious
problems for the plants they feed on, but sometimes many spittlebugs share
the same plant, which can cause damage.

African Gray Treefrog • *Chiromantis xerampelina*
Habitat: Savanna
Where: Southeastern tip of Africa • Length: 3 inches (7 cm)

Amazing Facts: A foam nest contains around 850 eggs, each about the size of the
head of a pin. The foam contains oxygen eggs need. The tadpoles drop from the
nest all at once. Nests are made at night and may take several hours to complete.

Pearl Gourami • *Trichogaster leeri*
Habitat: Rivers with many plants, often stagnant water
Where: Thailand, Malaysia, Indonesia • Length: 4 inches (10 cm)

Amazing Fact: Unlike most fish, which get oxygen from the water around
them, gouramis get oxygen from air breathed at the surface. So gouramis are
able to live in stagnant water with little oxygen, where other fish can't survive.
Bubble nests keep the gourami eggs near the surface, where oxygen is plentiful.

Human • *Homo sapiens*
Habitat: All kinds • Where: Worldwide

Amazing Fact: Ships go into drydock, a special docking pen, when they
need to be out of water for repairs. A bubble curtain at the entrance lets ships
enter, but keeps animals safely outside. Before bubble curtains, fish and seals
would swim into drydock with the ships, and then get stuck once the water
drained. Bubbles to the rescue!

GLOSSARY • INDEX

Scientists have a fancy word for everything!

They sure do.

Cool!

ACKNOWLEDGMENTS

I wish to thank the following scientists and scholars around the globe who answered all my questions; generously shared their research, labs, expertise, and experiences, as well as a few laughs and some critter-cam footage; and reviewed the manuscript:

Dr. Lance Barrett-Lennard and Jen Reynolds, Vancouver Aquarium Marine Science Centre; Dr. Jim Bodkin, Alaska Science Center, USGS; Dr. Gary Caldwell, Newcastle University, Newcastle upon Tyne, UK; Dr. Randall Davis, Texas A&M University at Galveston; Dr. Larry Dill, Simon Fraser University, and the Alaska-British Columbia Whale Foundation; Dr. Thomas Eisner, Cornell University; Dr. Andy Hamilton, Canadian National Collection of Insects, Arachnids and Nematodes; Chris Himes, the Burke Museum of Natural History and Culture, WA; Dr. Elaine Humphrey, University of British Columbia BioImaging Facility; Dr. Michael Jennions, the Australian National University; Andy Johnson, Monterey Bay Aquarium; Dr. Nancy Knowlton, Scripps Institution of Oceanography of the University of California, San Diego, and Smithsonian Tropical Research Institute; Dr. John F. Pagels, Virginia Commonwealth University; James Reyff, Illingworth & Rodkin, Inc., Acoustical Engineering; Dr. Paul Seldon, the Natural History Museum, London, UK; Dr. Michel Versluis, University of Twente, The Netherlands; Dr. Reese Voshell, Virginia Tech; Don White, Project Delphis; Dr. Terrie Williams, University of California, Santa Cruz.

Thank you to Carolyn for finding the perfect way to express the science, whimsy, and heart of my words; a bow to Roxyanne Young and Kelly Milner Halls, without whom this book could still be sitting in my Ideas File; and my thanks and love to Michael, Teri, Jonathan, and Dessa, the folks who share my bubble.